CRAYOLA
BOREDOM-BUSTING
CRAFTS

Rebecca Felix

LERNER PUBLICATIONS ◆ MINNEAPOLIS

The photographs in this book were created by Mighty Media, Inc.

Official Licensed Product
Lerner Publications Company
A division of Lerner Publishing Group, Inc.
241 First Avenue North
Minneapolis, MN 55401 USA

For reading levels and more information, look up this title at www.lernerbooks.com.

Main body text set in Mikado a 14/19.
Typeface provided by HVD Fonts.

Library of Congress Cataloging-in-Publication Data

Names: Felix, Rebecca, 1984– author. | Crayola (Firm)
Title: Crayola boredom-busting crafts / by Rebecca Felix.
Description: Minneapolis : Lerner Publications, 2019. | Series: Colorful
    Crayola crafts | Includes bibliographical references and index. | Audience:
    Ages 6–10. | Audience: K to Grade 3.
Identifiers: LCCN 2018015758 (print) | LCCN 2018028142 (ebook) |
    ISBN 9781541512528 (eb pdf) | ISBN 9781541511002 (lb : alk. paper) |
    ISBN 9781541545953 (pb : alk. paper)
Subjects: LCSH: Handicraft for children—Juvenile literature.
Classification: LCC TT160 (ebook) | LCC TT160 .F45723 2019 (print) |
    DDC 745.5083—dc23

LC record available at https://lccn.loc.gov/2018015758

Manufactured in the United States of America
1-43984-33998-7/27/2018

Contents

Craft Your Own Fun! 4

This to That Mural 6

Cheerful Fortune Cookies 8

Mosaic Puzzle 10

Story Scroll 12

Pull-String Puppets 14

Tiny Trunk Troupe 16

Colorful Window Art 18

Cardboard Castle 20

Paper Animal Costumes 24

Get Creative! 28
Glossary 30
To Learn More 31
Index 32

PAGE PLUS +

Scan QR codes throughout for step-by-step photos of each craft.

CRAFT YOUR OWN FUN!

Are you a maker? You can be! Follow the steps, and get busy creating fun crafts!

Let the photos and colorful materials inspire you. Then, dream up new details for each craft. Get ready to create some fun!

Crafting Safety

▶ **Being creative is fun.** But check with an adult before using a material or a tool in a new way to make sure it's safe to do so.

▶ **Keep workspaces clean** and free of clutter.

▶ **Work carefully** with paints and glues. Cover your work area first. Do not touch your face or eyes while using these materials. Wash your hands after use.

Boredom-Busting Tips

▷ Use your imagination. Art supplies can be used to create endless creations, from simple to those that will keep you busy for hours.

  ▪ Brainstorm how to make your craft different. Can you swap out missing materials for what you have on hand? Can you think of new uses for the craft or new ways to make it? Try it out!

▷ Have fun with mistakes.

  ▪ Did you complete a step in the wrong order? Is your craft not turning out? Have fun with it! Improvise. Make your mistakes into part of the craft. Or let them inspire you to make a whole new craft!

▷ Keep the fun going!

  ▪ Think of ways to extend or build on a finished craft. What else could you add?

  ▪ What other things could you make using the same idea or steps but different materials?

THIS TO THAT MURAL

Use your imagination to turn traced items into amazing art!

Materials

- everyday objects that can be traced
- pencil
- 11" x 17" paper
- markers
- crayons
- glue
- googly eyes
- colored poster board
- scissors

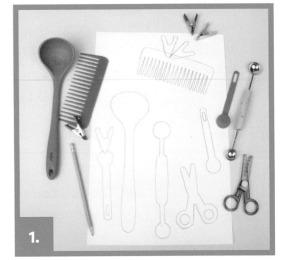

1.

1. Gather some objects from around your home or school such as a comb, scissors, or a plastic fork. Trace the items on the paper. There are a couple ways to do this.

2. One way is to start by tracing one shape. Decide what it will become. Then get inspired by the other items. Do traced scissors look like an alien body? Will traced clips look like wings? Get creative!

3. Another way is to begin by tracing all the items you gathered at once. Overlap tracings or place them randomly on the paper. Then decide what the shapes look like.

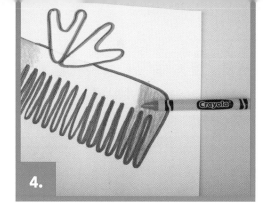

4. Use markers and crayons to complete your scene. Glue googly eyes to any creatures.

5. Glue the paper to the poster board. Cut near the paper edges to make a frame. Then hang up your work of art!

Scan code to see more photos!

CHEERFUL FORTUNE COOKIES

Create cute clay cookies that contain messages to family and friends!

Materials

- Model Magic
- rolling pin
- large chenille stems (pipe cleaners)
- fine line marker
- ribbon
- scissors
- clear tape

1. Roll a ball of Model Magic and flatten it with the rolling pin. Lay three chenille stems across the top.

1.

2. Gently fold the circle in half over the chenille stems. Then bend the chenille stems into a loop and twist their ends together.

3. Form the clay into a fortune cookie shape. Make sure the cookie edges are not too close together. Let the fortune cookie dry overnight.

2.

4. Carefully remove two large chenille stems from the cookie.

5. Write a nice message on a length of ribbon. Cut the ribbon so one end has plenty of blank space. Tape the blank end of the ribbon to one end of the chenille stem still inside the cookie. Slowly pull the ribbon through the cookie until the blank end is hanging out. Trim the ribbon.

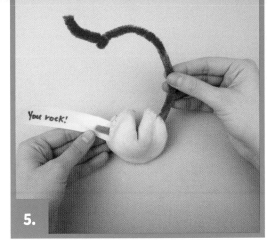

5.

6. Repeat steps 1 through 5 to make more cookies. Then give them to people to brighten their day!

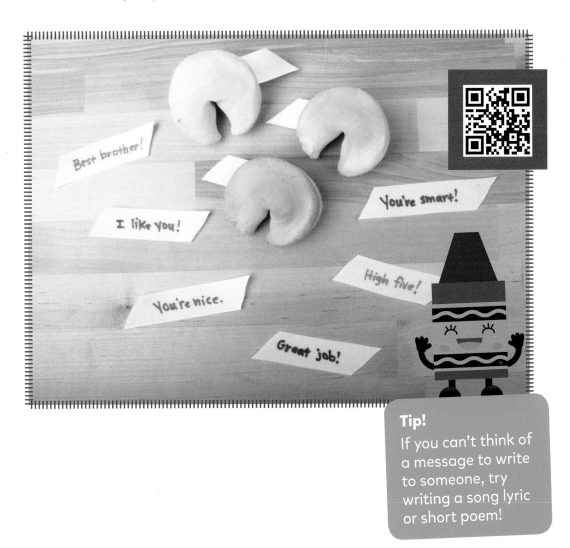

Tip!
If you can't think of a message to write to someone, try writing a song lyric or short poem!

MOSAIC PUZZLE

Mosaics are artworks made from small, colorful pieces formed into designs or patterns. Make your own mosaic in the form of a puzzle!

Materials
- rolling pin
- Model Magic in several colors
- plastic knife
- paint
- paintbrushes
- shoebox lid
- glue (optional)

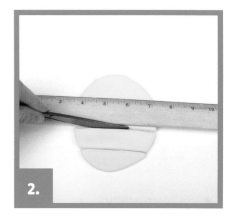
2.

1. Roll out the Model Magic into a large sheet about 1 inch (2.5 cm) thick.

2. Use the plastic knife to cut about 25 shapes. Let them dry overnight.

3. Paint the shoebox lid. Let the paint dry.

2a.

4. Your puzzle is ready to be arranged! Fit the clay pieces into the shoebox lid. Work to see how many you can fit. Or make a design. Try many combinations. If you create one you want to keep, glue the pieces in place on the lid. Or leave the pieces loose and design with them again and again!

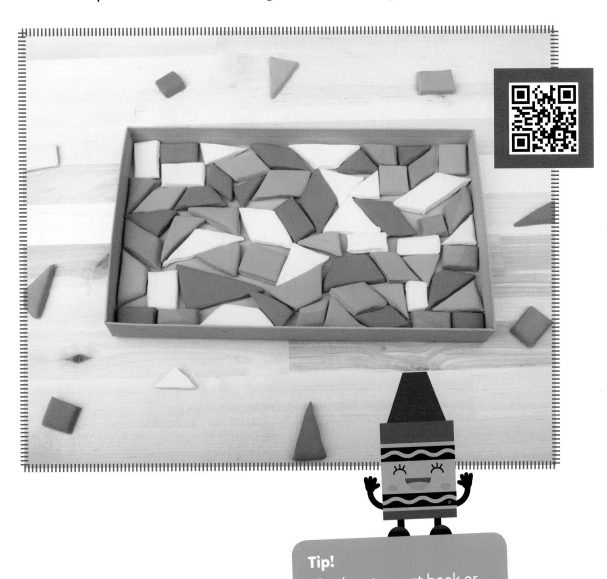

Tip!
Check out an art book or have an adult help you do online research for more information on what mosaic artwork looks like.

STORY SCROLL

People wrote stories in scrolls before books were invented. Use art supplies and your imagination to create your own scroll story!

Materials

- pencil
- notebook
- scissors
- paper
- clear tape
- construction paper
- crayons
- pen
- ribbon

1. Write a short story in a notebook. Then break up the story's words into pages.

2. Cut several pieces of paper in half lengthwise. Tape the paper halves together to create one long strip.

3. Roll a piece of construction paper into a tube, and tape it together. Repeat and set one tube aside. Tape the second tube along the paper strip's left edge.

4. Draw a rectangle on the paper strip for each page of your story. If you end up with extra paper at the end, trim it. If you run out of paper, repeat step 2 to make and add more strips. Tape the second tube to the end of the paper.

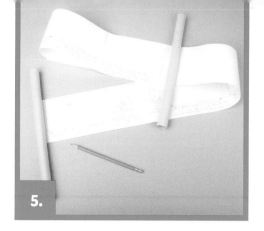

5.

5. Write the words of your story under the rectangles. Draw images to illustrate your story in the rectangles. Color the images, and go over the words in pen.

6. Roll the tubes together until they meet. Tie a ribbon around the scroll to keep it closed. To read the story, remove the ribbon and open the scroll panel by panel.

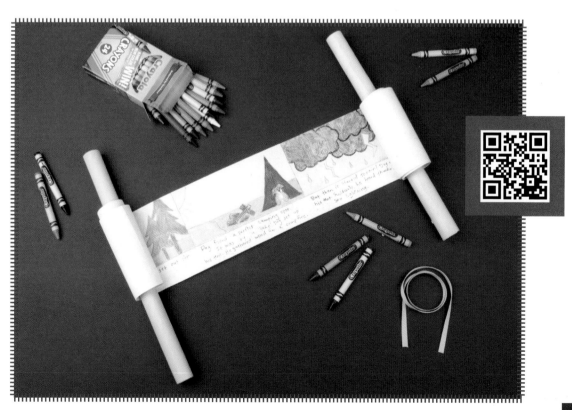

PULL-STRING PUPPETS

Make puppets that actually move!

Materials

- scissors
- cereal box
- pencil
- paint
- paintbrushes
- clear tape
- hole punch
- brass fasteners
- string

1. Cut the cereal box into a large sheet. Draw character or animal body parts on the cardboard. Cut out the shapes.

2. Paint the body shapes. Let the paint dry.

3. Tape the head to the body. Then punch one hole in the body for each arm, leg, ear, or wing. Punch two holes in the top of the head for the ears and one hole at the base of each arm and leg.

4. Use brass fasteners to connect the head and other body parts to the body through the holes. Flatten the ends of each fastener on the back of the puppet.

5. Cut one piece of string for each arm, leg, ear, or wing. Tape each string to a moving body part. Tie the other ends of the strings together.

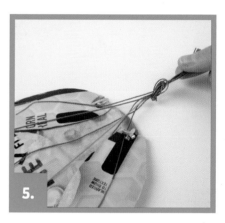

6. Hold the puppet by its bottom and its head string. Pull the puppet down, and watch it move!

TINY TRUNK TROUPE

Design a group of clay characters that travel in a trunk and put on plays!

Materials

- air-dry clay
- paint
- paintbrushes
- stickers
- markers
- glue
- construction paper
- scissors
- shoebox

1. Choose a theme for your trunk and troupe. This could be animals, traveling magicians, a ballet troupe, and more.

2. Create small clay characters. Let the clay dry overnight.

3. Paint the clay characters. Let the paint dry.

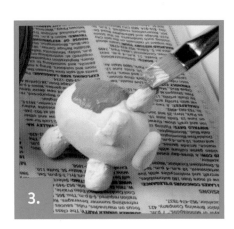

4. Use stickers, paint, markers, and glued-on construction paper to decorate the shoebox. Make it look like a traveling trunk.

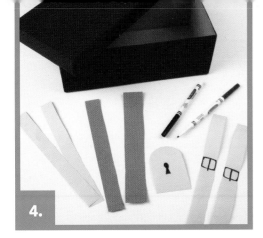

5. Create backgrounds from construction paper. These could include trees, a lake, stage, and more. Then put on mini plays with your tiny troupe!

COLORFUL WINDOW ART

Create a mini window with a bright design!

Materials

- wax paper
- newspaper
- paintbrushes
- glitter paint
- scissors
- washable school glue
- black construction paper
- clear tape
- yarn

2.

1. Tear out a piece of wax paper, and place it on newspaper.

2. Paint the wax paper with glitter paint, and let the paint dry.

3. Cut and glue together a window frame from black construction paper.

3.

4.

4. Glue the window frame to the wax painting. Trim the extra wax paper.

5. Tape a piece of yarn to the back of the frame. Then hang your artwork in front of a real window, and watch the colorful light shine through it!

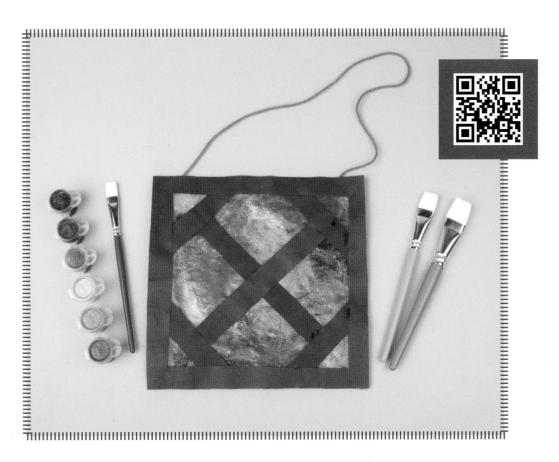

CARDBOARD CASTLE

Construct cardboard into an incredible castle!

Materials

- ruler
- pencil
- small cardboard box
- scissors
- duct tape
- 4 paper towel roll tubes
- newspaper
- paint
- paintbrush
- large cardboard box
- glue
- construction paper
- glue stick
- markers
- 4 wooden craft sticks

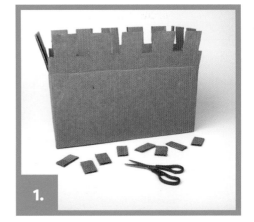

1. Use a ruler and pencil to draw towers along the top edges or flaps of the small box. Cut out the tower notches.

2. If the box has flaps, tape the inside corners together so the flaps stand up.

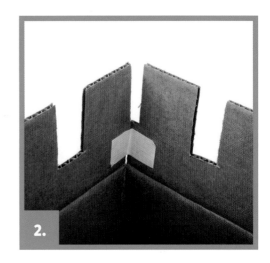

3. Cut out tower notches in one end of each paper towel roll tube.

4. Tape a paper towel roll to each corner of the box as towers.

5. Set the castle on newspaper and paint it. Let the paint dry.

6. Cut one flat side out of the large box. Glue several sheets of blue construction paper to it. This makes a moat.

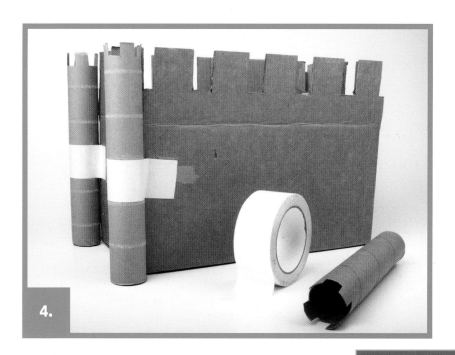

Cardboard Castle continued next page

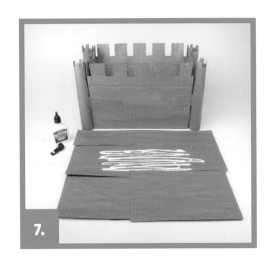

7.

7. Glue the bottom of the castle to the moat.

8. Cut a wide strip of green construction paper. Cut fringe along the edges. This is a grass bridge for the moat.

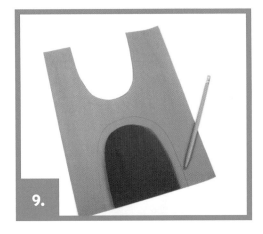

9.

9. Cut a door out of brown construction paper. Trace it on black construction paper, and cut out the shape. Glue the black shape to the leftover brown paper. Cut out around the shape to make a door frame. Use a marker to add wooden board details to the door and frame.

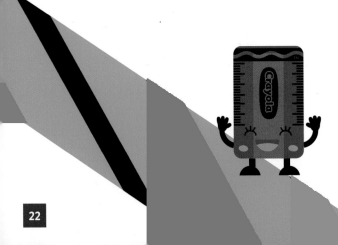

10. Make windows out of black and yellow construction paper.

11. Cut colorful flags from construction paper. Color the wooden craft sticks with markers. Glue one flag to each stick.

12. Glue one flag inside each tower. Glue the door frame and windows to the castle. Glue the grass to the moat and the door to the grass.

PAPER ANIMAL COSTUMES

Make cool costumes using construction paper, cardboard, and colorful art supplies!

Materials

Dinosaur Costume

- glue
- googly eyes
- baseball cap
- construction paper
- scissors
- duct tape

Cat Costume

- pencil
- construction paper
- scissors
- duct tape
- hard headband
- safety pin

Butterfly Costume

- pencil
- scissors
- cardboard
- paintbrush
- glue
- construction paper
- duct tape
- clear tape
- 2 stretchy headbands

Dinosaur Costume

1. Glue googly eyes to the front of the baseball cap.

2. Fold a piece of construction paper in half lengthwise, and cut spikes along its length. Repeat with several sheets of paper.

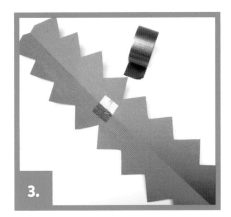

3. Unfold the papers. Tape the strips together to make one long strip. The strip can go down your back and to your feet as a tail!

4. Fold each row of spikes into the fold in the center to make a flat bottom along the strip. Then tape one end of the strip to the back of the baseball cap.

5. Cut several large triangles from the construction paper. Fold one edge to make a flap and tape the flaps to the underside of the baseball cap bill to make teeth.

Paper Animal Costumes continued next page

1.

2.

Cat Costume

1. Draw and cut out cat ears from construction paper.

2. Tape the ears to the top or sides of the headband.

3. Create an animal tail from construction paper. Have an adult pin it to the back of your shirt with a safety pin.

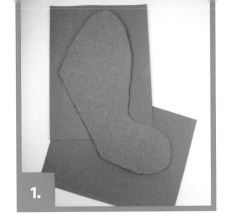

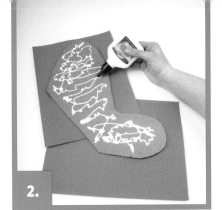

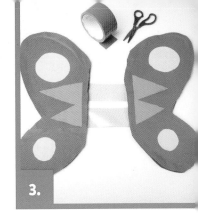

Butterfly Costume

1. Draw and cut out a large wing shape from cardboard. Trace the wing on cardboard, and cut out the second shape.

2. Brush glue onto both sides of the wings, and cover them in construction paper. Trim the extra paper around the wings.

3. Cut shapes from construction paper, and glue them onto the wings.

4. Use strips of duct tape to connect the wings.

5. Use clear tape to attach one headband on each side of the wing above the duct tape. Use these to wear your wings!

Tip!
Save old clothes and use them to create other costumes.

Get Creative!

After you've completed all these cool projects, think about what else you can create. There's no room for boredom when you use your imagination!

Find new ways to make each project your own. Try swapping construction paper for newspaper or paint for markers. Make a spooky monster costume, or build a whole kingdom made from cardboard! With colorful art supplies, the possibilities are endless.

Glossary

creative: skillful at using your imagination and thinking of new ideas

improvise: to create or achieve something with whatever is available

inspire: to influence and encourages someone to achieve something

moat: a deep, wide ditch dug around a castle and filled with water to prevent enemies from entering the castle

randomly: in a way that is without any order or purpose

scrolls: pieces of paper with writing on them that are rolled up into the shape of a tube

troupe: a group of theatrical performers

To Learn More

Books

Bernhardt, Carolyn. *Duct Tape Fashion*. Minneapolis: Lerner Publications, 2017.
Learn to make cool clothes, accessories, and costumes from colorful duct tape!

Devos, Sarah. *I Am Never Bored: The Best Ever Craft and Activity Book for Kids; 100 Great Ideas for Kids to Do When There Is Nothing to Do*. Beverly, MA: Quarry Books, 2018.
Find tons of crafts and activities featuring all kinds of topics and materials!

Uliana, Kim. *Crafting Fun for Kids of All Ages: Pipe Cleaners, Paint & Pom-Poms Galore, Yarn & String & a Whole Lot More*. New York: Sky Pony, 2017.
Browse through two hundred crafts, including those made for holidays, certain seasons, school, decoration, and just for fun!

Websites

Alien Scavenger Hunt
http://www.crayola.com/crafts/alien-scavenger-hunt-craft/
Looking for one more boredom-busting craft? Create alien names for small objects around your home. Then craft cool bags listing these names and have family or friends hunt for the items!

14 Crafts for When You Are Bored
https://alittlecraftinyourday.com/2014/08/27/14-crafts-for-when-you-are-bored/
Find photos and links to crafts that you can make with materials you have at home!

Index

cardboard, 14, 20, 24, 27, 28

clay, 8, 11, 16

crayons, 6–7, 12

duct tape, 20–21, 24–27

googly eyes, 6–7, 24–25

markers, 6–7, 8, 16, 20, 22–23, 28

materials, 4–5, 6, 8, 10, 12, 14, 16, 18, 20, 24

paint, 4, 10, 14, 16, 18, 20–21, 28

ribbon, 8–9, 12–13

safety, 4